The Bob Card
"I still don't trust anyone"
Volume 2
Pharmaceutical's finest....

Preface

People never cease to amaze me by some of their ridiculous actions. I am often in amazement at things that people say and do. This book will share several humorous stories from the field of pharmaceutical sales and doctor's offices. The doctors and their staff have shared stories with me from real sales representatives that call on their offices. No names are mentioned to protect the idiots and patient information. There are also a few new rules that needed to be added since my last book. The longer I stay in this business and it changes, more rules will be added to stay ahead of the Big Pharma system.

Table of Contents

1. The new visual aid
2. MR. E
3. Arrogant and Pushy
4. Medical Science Liaison/ Managed Care
5. Lunch Selections
6. Boss Ride Along
7. Does Sexy Sell?
8. Topic of Discussion
9. National Meetings
10. New Rules
11. Quirky doctors
12. It's all about the pay

The New Visual Aid

Have you ever seen a doctor glaze over like they are going to pass out? A sure way is to watch a pharmaceutical representative engage a doctor with an iPad visual aid. The visual aid in pharmaceuticals has gone through many changes in order to best capture the doctor's attention. Once you have their attention, the next step is to deliver a relevant point to encourage the doctor to prescribe your drug. This is what we have been told for years by the pharmaceutical marketing departments. They conjure up some study that validates how doctors want a message delivered to them. I have been in this business over 15 years and I have not yet had a doctor ask me for the "Hollywood" glossy visual aid or to view a pod cast to validate a point. 99% of the time we both dive into the PI, package insert, to find the FDA approved clinical data that they are seeking. The package insert is the most reliable and non-biased information that you can present to a doctor. The information is FDA approved and clinical, which is meat and potatoes to a physician.

Companies now are using the Ipad as a visual aid for two reasons. "It is so easy to operate" and "the company can track your every move".

The second quote was my theory on the real reason for Ipad use. My book, Volume 1, details of tracking the sales representatives. The problem with the Ipad is that many operations are too time consuming and still contain the cheesy marketing messages. The newest innovation from pharmaceutical marketing is the pod cast. The companies utilize approved physician speakers to deliver short message about the drug that the rep is promoting. This may be fine at a lunch or breakfast appointment, but in the sample closet is not the best time for this tool. I often joked with doctors in the past about watching a short film strip, because I knew they were crunched for time. Now through the genius of technology and the numbskulls of pharmaceutical marketing, it is a reality. My company requires updates periodically to the Ipad in order download the latest data about Ipad use in the field. This data includes information on how the tool is being utilized, which pages are most popular, and how long top performers are staying on each page. I click on pages occasionally as I speak with the doctor about fishing, vacations, and other personal information. Funny, I maintain top performance status without following the herd. Exactly! As much as pharmaceutical companies want to believe that their brilliant innovations and persuasive sales tactics are cause of success, it's simply selling a good drug from someone that understands that they are support, not the educator. I have even discussed my books with physicians and we laughed about them. Great detail! I am not deliberately a rebel against the company, but I do use common sense in my daily encounters with my customers. I put myself in the doctor's place when paying them a visit. Doctors are hip to the new technologies. Generally they clam up when walking towards a rep holding an Ipad. They know that this means cheesy detail time. In a survey I took, physicians clam up to the rep with an Ipad situation only second to seeing a Rep with a manager and an Ipad. UUGGGGHH!!! See, I can conjure up survey data as well. But the difference is, mine is actually true. 100% of the physicians I spoke with about this agreed that the Ipad details are cheesy and ineffective. Hey pharmaceutical marketing, put that in your pipe and smoke it! You guys are smoking something to think that your brainwashing slogans and cheesy ad campaigns are going to sell anything. Pharmaceutical marketing people are typically ex-reps that couldn't sell, but knew how to use other's work in a group setting to make themselves look good. So they weasel their way into a corporate marketing gig. Now they can implement cheesy slogans and marching orders to the sales force to increase sales. Unfortunately, the only increase is at the landfill as doctors and staff line the wastebasket. I love technology, but doctors do not want animation or slogans when choosing a therapy. Usually, it's facts about efficacy and side effects, but if you haven't sold anything yourself, you probably didn't get the memo. These are behind the desk types that have ideas that are not based in everyday reality. These are the geniuses that come up with team building activities that really build no trust and are boring unless you are in elementary school.

Mr. E

Common sense is valuable and useful, but if you lack it, you are a danger to yourself. An ex-colleague of mine is the topic of frequent mishaps in offices in my territory. I have stumbled into conversations about this guy, unsolicited , on several occasions in different locations. We will call this person Mr.E. While attending a speaker program at an Italian restaurant, I enjoyed a conversation with a doctor and nurse from my territory. Since it was October, the topic of Halloween came up. The nurse said to the doctor, " do you think he dress up at the office again this year?" , as the both shook their heads. The doctor says" who knows with that guy." Immediately, I flashback to an idea sharing meeting 2 years earlier when Mr. E said , " I often dress up as a famous western movie character in my offices and they seem to like it." Just as Mr. E finishes speaking, my phones rings to the whistling tune of a western movie and I said , " it's for you Mr. E!" And the room erupted in laughter. As I refocus in the present conversation with the doctor and nurse, I say, " is it Mr. E?" They look at me with amazement and say, "Do you know him?" And I told the story about our meeting. We laughed out loud and continued to laugh throughout the program. The doctor tells me that he will not see Mr. E at the office because he can't take a hint and overstays his welcome. I almost choke on a drink of water as the laughter continues. It really is a small world. The doctor asked how I knew Mr. E and said, " you can't make this stuff up!" He shakes his head and looks as though he has seen an alien aircraft.

    Mr. E uses his company provided data about the doctor's prescribing habits in an office. This is a big "no go" in pharmaceuticals. All doctors know we have the information, but you never share it with the doctor. They don't like feeling like big brother is monitoring their treatment habits, etc. Also, the data is only about 60% accurate. So Mr. E goes to an appointment with his list and decides it's a good idea to ask the doctor why he has 75 patients and only 3 on his drug. The doctor said,"excuse me." As the doctor peers over the rim of his glasses as he looks at Mr. E and continues to write in his patient's chart, Mr. E doubles down with his original statement. The doctor said" the last time I checked my name has an MD after it, not yours and these are my patients." The doctor walks away and goes the the front receptionist and said, " he is kicked out, cancel all lunches and no appointments!" Three months later Mr. E went back into the office and begged forgiveness with a tear in his eye. The doctor was gracious and allowed him back in with a stern warning not to do that again. This didn't have to happen. He listened to his boss, who has never sold anything in his life. He couldn't sell a hooker on a troop train.

Could Mr. E have more stories? Oh yeah! Another office in the northern part of the territory was a closed office. Which means no appointments, lunches, or programs. The office decided to allow one pharmaceutical lunch per week, each Monday. The receptionist likes me so she called and offered me a couple of lunches. On my appointment, I was informed that the books were closed and the remainder of the year was booked. I could not believe it. I thanked her for the lunches that she gave me and went on my way. Later that day the receptionist called me with a new discovery. She said" some guy named Mr. E booked 2 lunches per month for the entire year." I began to laugh to myself. She asked if I knew him. I replied" all too well." She said he was weird and annoyed her. I asked how. She said, " he stands at the window and stares at us until we let him go back to see the doctor ." I have a gift of being able to sound like other people. So I used this gift to have some fun. I called the receptionist and pretended to be Mr. E. She left me on hold for 15 minutes. When she finally answered the phone, I was greeted with contempt in her voice. I asked in Mr. E's voice, " why did you cancel my lunches? Who do you think you are?" I knew her blood was boiling, but I laughed out loud and she recognized my laugh. She said, "I'm gonna get you good!" As she laughed as well. We still laugh about that with the staff when I visit the office.

Mr. E places high value into the marketing material that the office provides for you. He takes brain washing to a new level. Once he has spilled the talking points on the doctor and staff, he strategically places leave behind marketing pieces around the office for the doctors and staff to view. 5-10 pieces on the coffee maker, in the refrigerator, on the wall, in the food line. Literally everywhere! I watched a staff member say, " Mr. E has been here", as he collected the pieces and threw them in the garbage. The doctor and nurse at this office refer to Mr. E as Lurch. The nurse said that she text the doctor during the lunch with Mr. E and said, "Don't leave!" The doctor snickered and said, " thanks for lunch" as he headed out of the lunch area. He smiled at the nurse on the way out the door. She was furious that he left her alone with Mr. E. Although she doesn't have any part in the process of Mr. E's drug, he will still give her the FULL detail. She just wanted to enjoy her 30 minute lunch break and unwind a little. Sometimes it pays to know when to back off and try again another day.

My favorite Mr. E story is when he was asked to ride along with a new female rep in the another area. He agrees and travels done to territory of the new rep for the ride along. The next day they made many calls together. At the end of the day the unthinkable happens. Mr. E, who is only a sales rep, tells the new girl that she is awful pulls her out of the field. What? By what authority? Yes, he pulls her out of the field and tells her that she needs to be re- trained. He sends an email to her boss and the training people explaining what he did with the new rep. To make matters worse, in this day of diversity and political correctness, it was a black female rep, who just came off of maternity leave. She probably used common sense and made great connections with the offices, but Mr. E is a marketing man, and that makes her efforts null and void. You would think that he finally stepped into a crap hole too deep to recover. However, nothing happened to him and he is still employed by the same company. Nothing really surprises me anymore!

Can I have your next 5 patients doc?

Arrogant and Pushy

There are many in the pharmaceutical business with a problem of arrogance. Endless is the number of people that I have worked with that think they are the smartest person in the room. Among these are the Elite arrogant that think arguing with a doctor about a study or drug data is a good idea. Remember, we as reps went to a 2 week course on the drug. The doctors went to 10 years of school, certifications, clinical experience, and are well read on the latest therapies. But arrogance is often blinding. An example of this is a guy in my territory we will call Motorcycle man. Yes, he gained the name from riding a motorcycle to work. Samples and iPad in his saddlebags, in a suit and off to work on his motorcycle. A young doctor was asking about a particular study with Motorcycle man's drug. As motorcycle man explained the data to the doctor, the doctor pointed out flaws in the study design. So after a few minutes of this happening at a lunch, the conversation escalates. The nursing staff and others at the lunch said the motorcycle man took great offensive to the doctor's view of his companies study. He took so much offense that he challenged the doctor' Integrity with his patient's. Never a good idea! The doctor smiled and said when you can bring me something clinically significant, I will see you again. The motorcycle man was obviously angry, by his facial expression. He left the lunch and sped off on his motorcycle. The doctor knew that he had motorcycle man and would not give in. This is where common sense plays a great part. Most doctors have participated in clinical studies and understand study designs and desired outcomes. As reps, we have not participated in any clinical trials. This is a great place for us to learn from the doctors and gain from their expertise. I believe arrogance is blind to common sense.

Another example is from a lady in my territory, who is known for being excessively pushy with the doctors and staff. We will call her Maude. She was a little older than the average rep and overcompensated for her age difference by being very pushy and controlling. A doctor that I am friends with said that she writes a lot of this reps drug each week, probably 15-20 prescriptions. Monday morning comes around and Maude came in to see this doctor. In a hallway call, which is typically 30 seconds to 2 minutes, Maude attempts to read an entire study, word for word, to the doctor. The doctor and nurse look at each other and laugh., " It's Monday morning, do you think I have time to read a study while seeing patients?" She takes the study and says, "I'll read it later." The rep then says will you put your next 5 patients on Nopain? The doctor says "Sure," and laughs as she walks away. I happen to have lunch with the doctor that day and she told me the story. We both laughed. Then the doctor said, " I have written my "quota" of 5 Nopain this morning, I guess I'll write a different drug for the other patients with that condition the rest of the week." We laughed harder. The doctor said," Never give the doctor a quota!" Although she was joking about writing a different drug for her other patients, she made a valid point. Maude could have cheated herself out of 10-15 scripts due to her lack of respect for the doctor's time. The office staff can't stand Maude and, actually cancelled a few of her lunches and offered them to me and other reps. Fortunately, Maude took an early retirement and many offices were relieved that she would not be returning to their office.

Shake that money maker......or not!

Medical Science Liaisons/Managed Care

The medical side of pharmaceutical sales is similar to the CIA or seal team in the military. They don't tell anyone what they are doing or how, but they get the job completed and nobody knows how until after the mission is completed. I have a friend in medical and she operates in stealth mode, specializes in being undetected. Medical handles questions about off label use of a drug, information about studies, and medical society updates. The sales side of the business is not allowed to access this information. One morning I had breakfast with my top doctor and we were talking football before the breakfast arrived. Out of nowhere, the receptionist joined us and said to me, " your MSL is here." I asked why. She said he wanted to update the doctor on a recent case, but the doctor was already in the know. The doctor said, " I'll give him 5 minutes." He asked me to meet him in the break room and I agreed. Later the doctor comes in the break room and I could tell there was something wrong. He spoke for a few minutes and left to see patients. After I left the office the nurse calls me to tell me what happened with the MSL. While waiting on the doctor the MSL decides to look in a patient file that was laying on the counter in front of him. The doctor rounds the corner and said, " what in the hell are you doing? Ever hear of HIPPA? I know you are Medical, but you don't practice in this office! Get the Hell

Out!!" This explains why the doctor was off when he came in to see me at breakfast. The MSL, we will call Skippy. Skippy had other issues with other offices. He gelled his hair into a frohawk. His wardrobe was less than professional. He wore paisley shirts that were brightly colored with slacks, and untucked. When I saw this I was shocked! He looked an actor out of an 80's science fiction movie. Who dresses like this even at a dance club? Anyhow, the doctor made a phone call and he was fired for the incident in the doctor's office. I'm not the sharpest tool in the shed, but what made him think that was a good idea?

      My most desired job in pharmaceuticals is the managed care position. I don't think they have a job description in writing. Nobody, including management knows what these guys do. My managed care guy is like a good politician, full of crap. He never directly answers your concerns, but always promises to get back with you with the information you requested. These guys have relationships with the insurance companies about the placement of drugs on their formulary. What documentation is required and what the cost will be to the patient are frequent questions the managed care people receive. The insurance companies typically meet quarterly, semi annual , or annually, so they really don't have much to do. Their pay does not reflect their lack of activity. My mentors have told me this is their dream job for me in pharmaceuticals. These people have great tans, catch a lot of fish, coach their kids teams, and have great golf scores. Get my drift? It's a cake place to be in the industry. A managed care guy I had at another company on covered the VA. We meet with him annually. So this guy gave us the same update form every meeting for 4 years with no changes. Unless your drug company is willing to give everything away, the VA is probably not going to have your drug on formulary. VA is primarily generic driven. He looked to be at the gym a great amount of the time and had a golden tan. What a great place to be! I am in training for this job right now. I work Monday- Thursday until 2pm and make my numbers. Soon, I will be moving to the grand desired side of the business.

 I recently left a company and went with a start up company. Upon my arrival and completion of training, I discovered that my MSL at the new company is Mr. Frohawk. I was asked not to bring him in a couple of offices. You can't make this stuff up.

 Only one MSL has been valuable to me. She is a friend and has great relationship skills. Also, I trust her , so I have no fear of her going out with my offices. Since we can't take docs out anymore, it's nice to have a trusted person stand in the gap for you. Thanks CG.

Shake it! Don't break it!

Lunch Selections

Pharmaceutical reps are given generous allowances to feed offices and obtain time to educate the offices on their drug. An industry wide allowance of $25 per person in the office for breakfast and lunch is observed by most companies. Although each year I complete a projected budget for the year, I have never been held to those figures. Each year in the summer, I check in with my boss on my spending. Each time the same result. " you keep spending and I'll let you know when to stop." Not a problem! I overspend every year with no consequence. It's a requirement to spend in these offices. I usually call a catering company that will deliver. I don't cart food around unless it's for my favorite offices. In light of this, there's a guy in my territory that goes to the grocery store and buys bread, cold cuts, condiments and chips...EVERYDAY! This is all he brings to offices. He is known as the Sandwich guy! The offices didn't mind at first, but then people made subtle hints about his menu. He brings the same thing every lunch and at the end of lunch, he takes the leftovers home. Really! Not only cheap, but rude. I bet his family has an extra refrigerator to hold all of the cold cuts and condiments. To my surprise, this guy is actually a good rep and has done very well in the territory. He obviously didn't read my first book and the chapter on getting points or rewards from the catering company. The grocery doesn't give any kind of rewards. Hey guy, you are being talked about because you are cheap, with the company's money!

    A lady rep in my territory used Ruby Tuesday for catering. With each of the meals she ordered they added steamed broccoli to her order by request. She apparently liked broccoli, so she had the restaurant add it. If you have ever smelled steamed broccoli then you will understand what happened next. One day while seeing patients, the doctor, nurses, and patients were complaining about the stench in the office hallways. After investigating the situation, the doctor found that broccoli was included in the lunch back in the break room. The entire office smelled like a portable toilet. The doctor removed the broccoli from the office break room and began to spray air freshener around the office. When the rep arrived for lunch she was puzzled as to why the catering company forgot the broccoli. The doctor and staff didn't like this lady. They felt that she was often rude and condescending. The doctor didn't tell her she threw the broccoli out, but instead informed her that nobody really liked broccoli in the office. After calling the catering company and discovering that the broccoli was delivered, she got the hint not to order it again.

    A good friend of mine was with his new boss for the day. Lunch time rolled around and they decided to eat at a popular Mexican restaurant. The lunch was great and both commented on how they enjoyed it. Part of my friend's job is carrying and storing drug samples for the doctor's offices. As a result the manager is required to check his samples and the place of storage to conduct an inventory. They proceeded to my friend's home and the unthinkable happened next. My friend went to his car to grab some additional samples and his boss asked for the restroom. He thought nothing of it, as it was probably just number one. When he returned from his car, to his surprise, an explosion occurred in his power room. That's right! His boss took a dump in his house. Who does that to a subordinate? My friend said he heard a bowel explosion, the fan running and a lot of spraying. I can only imagine what he was thinking as the cascade of noises came from the powder room. Apparently the Mexican food was wonderful! My friend hears the door being opened and immediately acts like he's counting sample boxes to avoid the awkwardness. Everything was fine, but in his head he was saying, " I can't believe that just happened in my home!" When he told me I laughed in the same amazement as my friend. Wow!

    A boss that I used to have was addicted to sugar. This guy looked at cookies like a tiger looks at his prey before he consumes it. I recall at a meeting once he ordered a snack for the group from the hotel catering service. They came and set up a nice display of cookies, fruit, nuts, and coffee. I notice the manager, Mr. L, hovering around the snack display with eyes fixed on the cookies. He said, " you guys come get some of these cookies before I do." When we returned to our seats to resume the meeting, Mr. L was sitting next to me. I'm not so sure if he was taught about chewing with his mouth closed, because he smacked those cookies so loud that it was disrupting the meeting. He is the boss, with a Napoleon complex, so who is going to put their job at risk. Nobody! So we continue the meeting with that moist smacking noise right in my ear. I looked over and said, "how are the cookies?" "Great!! Go get you some!" He replied. " That's a great idea!" I replied. Everyone knew that I was poking at the boss about the the smacking, but he was clueless. I got up and left the room, as if I were getting cookies, to get a break from the constant smacking sound.

  At the same meeting, Mr. L grabbed some hard candy that was sitting in the middle of the table. I thought that may be a quieter solution to his sugar fix. Boy, was I mistaken. It was louder than the smacking. I pinched myself to see if I was really there listening to this racket. He made sure that the hard candy hit every tooth in his mouth for the maximum sound effect. Lesson learned. At the next meeting, I came in extra early to get a seat far away from Mr. L. I also placed some hard candy on the table right in front of where he was sitting for extra entertainment factor. As long as it's not directly in my ear, I can enjoy the entertainment.

  The funniest lunch that a rep brought to an office was Crystal hamburgers. Cheap and nasty. If you have more money, which we do, do something nice for the office. Don't feed that something that will strap them to the John for the afternoon. I ate Crystal hamburgers in college because I was on a low income, and always on a night of drinking beer. I've never been to their restaurant in daylight. I laughed uncontrollably when the nurse told me about this. It still cracks me up that someone in the professional world thought that frat house beer munchies would serve well as a lunch at a doctors' office.

The boss ride along

When the boss rides along with a sales rep in pharmaceutical sales it's a two part outcome. One is so the boss can evaluate your relationships with the office and the other is to add value to the office. Adding value would include taking care of obstacles that the rep may not be able to handle in getting a patient on drug. Calling in the big guns, so to speak. The objective is not for the boss to sell your customers. Especially true of my ex-boss, known as Mr. L, the sugar addict.

Mr. L would get in the office and appear harmless and very friendly, until he was in front of the doctor. It was as if the limelight was upon him and this alter ego came alive. Mr. L had a successful sales career and had been successful as a manager, but I scratch my head as to why. This guy embarrassed everyone in his district with his gimmick sales lines that he would use on our doctors.

Mr. L was a short man with a severe case of Napoleon Syndrome. When he first met our tall, male nurse, he didn't have a chance to gain favor with Mr. L. Our nurse drove up to meet Mr. L in a new company vehicle that was nicer than Mr. L's. "How did you get that? It's better than mine and I'm a manager!" stated Mr. L. Immediately, the nurse was at a disadvantage with this guy. Later in the conversation they discussed the career path for the nurse. He expressed his interest in pursuing a management position with the company. The idea was immediately smashed by Mr. L. He said, "I don't think you have what it takes to be in management, you are inflexible." The nurse was floored that a man that has never met him before or worked with him would have this opinion of him. I told the nurse that it was because he was tall. We laughed, but there was a lot of truth to that statement. Every time the nurse took Mr. L into offices, a great story came out of the visit.

Once while visiting our largest customer, the nurse was talking with the doctor about how he could best support his office. During the conversation Mr. L says to the doctor, " I know I'm brainwashed, but we have a pearl of a drug!" You could have pushed the nurse over with a feather, and he is 6'6! The nurse thought, " who uses a cheesy line like that anywhere?" Dazed and embarrassed, the nurse took Mr. L back to his car and immediately called me to share this discovery. We wrote it off to a one time stupid occurrence.

Our district had a meeting and all of Mr. L's reps got together. In passing conversation, we uncovered many other instances when Mr. L use his " sales skills". It was now revealed, the used car salesman in Mr. L comes out on every field visit with us. Our Doctors found the cheesy sales pitch of the manager to be humorous, but we were usually embarrassed. At the meeting, over a couple of beers, the team would share stories about Mr.

L, while my partner and I would attempt a live imitation. This is always good for a good night of laughs.

    I remember one of the last ride alongs with Mr. L, we went to an office that is usually a short, to the point visit. This doctor is very busy and is short staffed, so there was no time for chit chat. As the doctor approaches, I greet him and gave him a quick update of the newest information, he thanks me and attempts to walk away. Instead, Mr. L says " I know I'm brainwashed, but ain't it great!" The doctor cuts eyes at me and walks away with no reply. Inside, I wanted to leave and never come back. It was like being a child and your parents say something "sweet" that embarrassed me. Because of Mr. L, I developed a warning and apology tour. I give the offices a heads up that the boss is with me and come back to apologize after the call. The last thing I want to do is be perceived as a guy that wastes people's time with a dog and pony show.

    Mr. L eventually unveiled his sales tactics in front of our Regional director. This guy is no- nonsense, sales oriented, numbers focused guy. During a area meeting, Mr. L joined a deep discussion about our product. He said to the group, " you all know that I'm brainwashed and have drank the koolaid and I believe that our drug is a pearl of a drug!" I immediately bit my lip to keep from laughing and glanced at the regional director for his response. His eyebrows raised and he was obviously taken back by these remarks. Two weeks later, we received notice that Mr. L decided to take early retirement from the company. 33 years isn't exactly early retirement, but needless to say, he was history. It's my belief that his wonderful sales speech at the area meeting nailed his coffin shut.

My current boss is old school pharmaceuticals. He speaks in codes with a look and a nod to confirm any questions in the gray area. I like him, but he plays the game of corporate messaging. That is one of his flaws in my opinion. Probably his biggest flaw was launching a fart at a lunch with me. Nobody had shown up to lunch, so the boss stepped out to "wash his hands", and when he returned, he brought a smelly friend. I didn't notice at first because people were beginning to come in and I was across the room. When I returned to my seat, I caught a whiff of that bomb and tried to ignore it. The girls in the lunchroom finally said what is that smell. Fortunately, they blamed it on the broccoli from yesterday's lunch and I was spared embarrassment. On my next visit one of the girls knew that he farted. She mentioned it to me and we erupted in laughter. She was being nice and I'm sure the boss appreciated that gesture. I bet a cold sweat ran down his back and a sigh of relief came over him , as the poor broccoli was blamed for his foulness.

NOT A RIDE ALONG, JUST KILL ME!!!!!

Does Sexy sell?

Most of the reps in the field are female. Many of them are quite attractive. I have always thought that sexy refers to someone who is beautiful and dresses somewhat form fitting and less revealing. Some female reps didn't get that coaching, as their dress code came from a risqué night club.

At a national meeting, we were introduced to our new VP of sales. When she took the stage, I was expecting a pole that she could spin on the be dropped as well. A true blonde with obvious enhancements steps on the stage in a skin tight dress. My jaw dropped. Not because Barbie (her nickname) was so desirable, but because I was sure that she was going to have a wardrobe glitch and pop out of that dress. She pace the stage and talked to us with the new brainwashing message, in high heels of course. She was definitely ready for a night in the town. I spoke to her in passing about an idea that I wanted to share about a current procedure. Half drunk, she pushed me off until the next day, as the dance floor awaited her. I like her energetic spirit, but the striptease meeting needs to go.

During a team building event at another meeting we played kick ball. That's right! We are treated as children much of the time, but it pays well. Everyone was advised to wear athletic attire, such as shorts and a t-shirt. My boss, nurse and I were making small talk as we waited to begin the game. My nurse nudged me to look at our boss. His eyes were about to pop out of his head. An older lady next to us was sitting on the bench putting on her sneakers. She was surgically enhanced up top and wore very tight shirts. This event was no different. However, her shorts were very loose. She straddled the bench with a knee up tying her shoe and the bottoms of her shorts were on the side revealing more than anyone wanted to see. My nurse and I cracked up that the boss' voice did not change when he saw this, but his eyes had extreme visual stimulation. He finally turned away. The nurse and I stepped away to laugh uncontrollably. Our boss didn't stay for an extended view, but I believe he was in shock at the view. I know that I was scarred by that view.

    I have a rep in my area that is known in many offices as CT. She has a really great personality and is very friendly. Most days she wears pants suits to work. These suits tend to be on the tighter side. Some of you have probably figured out the nickname by now. Yes, it's Camel Toe. Many offices have this same nickname for her. As well as she is liked, I am surprised that someone hasn't pulled her aside and made her aware of this situation. I wouldn't want that responsibility, would you? Also, since so many of her clothes are like this, do you think that maybe she knows or likes that style? Either way, she wears clothes that fit her in this way and even the doctors talk about it. I wonder if she sells a feminine product? If so it would make since that maybe she is doing a little extra advertising.

National Sales Director. Years in pharmaceutical industry, 8.

Topic of discussion

Most all of the large pharmaceutical companies are like the government. They are so politically correct that it's tough to hold a conversation. So many topics are out of bounds these days in a corporate work environment. Topics like sexual gender, religion, race and culture, and politics are out of bounds at my company. My best friend is black, or African-American. Give me a break! We are old school and call each other by the old self identifiers. He and I like to cut up and make people think we are divided and may get out of hand, but then we hug and laugh together and watch the victims of our jokes squirm. We have fun with that. Many of the doctors that I call on are old school too as far as being politically correct.

Once at a lunch program, my boss and 3 doctors attended to listen to our speaker. After the program concluded, we had an interesting conversation about a mystery patient of one of the attending doctors. The patient revealed to the doctor that she gets her anus bleached on a regular basis. The room went totally silent. "She does what?", says another doctor. The first doctor repeated himself and the room erupts in laughter. " I don't know what to say! ", says the other doctor. Apparently she is a very high maintenance patient that has too much time and money on her hands. I guess doctors discover all types of personal and unwanted information during exams with patients. I am still bewildered that someone thought that bleaching their anus was a good idea!

My favorite doctor told me about a patient he accepted as a favor to another doctor. The doctor accepted the patient on a one time basis to monitor them while taking a new therapy for their condition. The nurse met the patient in the lab and drew blood and took vitals. While the patient was waiting on the results in the patient room, she and her partner decided to engage in sexual intercourse. The nurse went to the patient room to report the lab results to the patient and walked in on a scene out of a porn movie. Her eyes bugged out, she turned out of the room and said, "Oh Lord!" I guess they finished what they started and the woman went into the hall and found the nurse. The nurse said , "I was coming to give you the lab results." The woman got the information and went back to the patient room. A while later the staff noticed an unusual fragrance in the hallway. It seemed to be coming from the restroom. No, it was not a bodily function producing the aroma. It was the guest patient and her friend in the restroom smoking marijuana. After the couple left the restroom together, the nurse wanted in to a cloud of pot smoke. She turned on the fan and began to spray air freshener to cover the smell. Angry with the couple, the nurse walked into the see the guest patients and informed them that the way that they were acting was not acceptable in their office. After the nurse informed the doctor about the situation, the doctor joined me for lunch and told me. We laughed hard and joked about the referring doctor. He said, " I need to reach out and thank him for the referral." Joking of course, we laughed about the nurses reaction to the situation.

The National Meetings

Without fail there is drama at most national meetings. Most time the open bar and excessive alcohol consumption by many proves to be a snare. We have a lady in our division that is high maintenance, many actually. She she is in her late forties, has several body enhancements, and shares way too much information. Also, she consumes a lot of alcohol at these meetings and usually ends up dancing and acting wild. She met a guy at one of the meetings that was married and they ended up roommates for the nights of the meeting. Public displays of affection were noticed from the two at several meetings. So we can say that they became an item at meetings.

One meeting, the cougar found a new, younger guy at the meeting to drink some beers and dance with her. The married guy was not happy about this, as displayed on his face. He pulled the cougar aside and apparently checked on their status together. Upset after the conversation, the married guy departed the area. The cougar went back to drinking and dancing with the new guy. A couple of hours later the married guy shows up and decides to have a few more words with the cougar. The new guy didn't like this guy blocking his chances with the cougar. Some colorful words were exchanged and an actual fight erupted on the dance floor. It was quickly broken up by bystanders. It was late enough that not very many people saw the fight. The fact that the married guy, the cheating dirtbag, decided to fight over his hook up and risk a six figure job is beyond me. My friends found out from eye witnesses and the funny text started. It was funny how stupid all three of them were that night. The new guy must have been desperate because the cougar is not attractive. The married guy has other obligations and put a lot at risk. The cougar was rolling the dice and seduced a guy who was better looking than she was pretty. It looks like the cougar got the best end of the deal.

Pharma companies have become more conservative in the places that they host national meetings. Las Vegas was a popular spot until many people lost control and made poor choices. At a meeting in Las Vegas, we had a couple of new people that joined the team. They were in the same training class and became friends. One night we had a free night on the town. Most people grab a few friends, get dinner and maybe a couple of drinks, at least the smart ones. Others like the new people decide to stay out all night or very late. That is self torture knowing that you will need to be engaged at the meeting. The two new guys thought they were still at the frat house in college. They started drinking after we were released for the day, about 5pm. Nobody saw the two of them all night. We showed up at the meeting room the next morning only to notice that two people were missing. Yes, the two new guys. The manager asked us to call them, but no answer. Next the manager sent someone up to their rooms to get them up. The hotel manager ended up opening the rooms and they were nowhere to be found. Now it was serious. The manager is now worried about the safety of these reps. He informed the regional director and they discussed the situation. After the meeting with the regional director, the manager walks through the casino where we stayed headed back to the meeting rooms. It was 8:30 and the meeting started at 8am. The manager glances over at a roulette tablet to see the two reps. They were dressed in yesterday's clothes, minus the tie and sleeves rolled up. They both had drinks in hand and were betting the table. The manager was relieved and angry. He walked over to the reps and said," what's going on? Why aren't you at the meeting?" They replied, " we wanted to take today off." The manager is floored by that stupid answer. He informed the regional manager of the discovery of the two reps. You know it's funny, I didn't see them again that meeting. Needless to say, they were both fired. I was floored that two people would throw away a six figure job for a night of fun in Vegas. This time what happened in Vegas, followed them home, it didn't stay in Vegas.

Call mama, we've got some drama!

New Rules

In general, flying under the radar is a good thing. The only time you should expect recognition is when your numbers are good. Otherwise you are inviting a lot of busy work and attention that will consume your time. If there is no additional money, why waste your time. These companies want you to do everything for as little as they can get away with paying you. We make a fraction of what the company and executives make and we do all of the work.

Making yourself too available to the manager is a mistake. If he/she recognize that you are readily available by phone, email, or in person, believe that they will use that to their advantage. The problem is that middle management is the worst job in pharmaceuticals. The busy work doesn't usually pay dividends, unless you are trying to get promoted into management. Some people like titles, but I'm in this for the money.

Manage the Manager. Also, the managers aren't looking out for your best interest, but their's. If you ask them about being promoted or anything that requires them to hire someone, don't expect genuine help. Hiring people in Pharma is a lengthy and cumbersome process, so the managers aren't eagerly rushing into interviews. Seldom answer your phone, answer emails, or offer assistance without a time delay, like you learned in my last book, the **three**

hour rule. Return calls after a 3 hour delay and hopefully they have already found someone to accomplish the busy task at hand.

Cover the camera on your company mobile devices. I have been told that your camera can be activated without your consent. I would not put it past a pharmaceutical company to access the camera during a speaker program or a lunch and learn to hear or see you doing something wrong. Remember, they are not trying to find you doing the right thing and with many gray areas at hand, it's best to be safe. Also, these companies are control freaks and always forget that we actually work about 1 hour per day. (About 10 minutes per doctor) many times they forget that there are 7 other work hours to fill during a day. Once I do my job, the rest of the day is mine. That's why we got into an outside sales job, for flexibility in our schedule.

Enter your activities at the last minute. Activities like speaker programs are monitored by the compliance people at the company. The more notice you give, the greater your chances of receiving a call that you will have an auditor at your event. Have you ever been called by the IRS? This is the pharmaceutical version. I have been audited after a program. I was questioned about things that were outside my control. I followed all of the rules, but I was treated as a murderer at a trial in whose hand they found on the bloody murder weapon. This includes daily calls. Some corporate people have been known to call the offices about your visits. Again, I have nothing to hide, but it's like paying taxes, we all do it, but we do not want a visit from the IRS.

- **Keep your resume updated and <u>circulating</u>**. Unfortunately, in this business of companies merging daily, drug patents being challenged, and the natural threat of the patent expiration, there's no room getting too comfortable in one position. There is always a potential threat of being jobless. Beat the system and always be open to new opportunities and challenges. The people that don't adapt to change are the ones that are looking for a job, instead of the of the one that landed a new one.

- **Don't get too comfortable in a position-** in pharmaceutical sales you are up against a clock, the patent life. Although many companies extend the patent life of a drug by making it extended release or controlled release , you truly have around 3-4 years to make money. You don't want to be around when the restructuring begins. Stay on top of the situation and leave by your own accord. The easiest thing to do is stay in a position, but that isn't always the smartest move.

- **Stay out of company gossip-** it's always good to know what's going on around you, but also understand the source behind information before considering it credible. Cafe Farma is not a credible site! It's a bitch session for miserable people that will not be happy at any company. The information on this site is about 30-40% accurate. Mostly BS. Misery loves company for sure. Check out the threads on these sites and you will understand. Avoid the groups with loud mouth reps that cause problems. Believe me, Pharma has a lot of loud mouth, self absorbed people. When the boss asks about situations fishing for information, tell them nothing! Stay low maintenance in their eyes. Management typically doesn't want to deal with petty situations, so avoid at all cost.

- **Plan personal trips in conjunction with company travel-** most meetings are at cool locations. Fort Lauderdale, Miami, New York, and Las Vegas are a few meeting spots that I have attended. However, you rarely get to enjoy the location due to the meeting. They keep you busy from 7am-10pm. Come in early or stay after the meeting to enjoy the location. The flights are covered , do the most you would pay is for additional nights for the room.

- **Avoid Buffets-** too many people touch the utensils at meetings. I'll see someone that I witnessed not washing their hands in the restroom scooping some mashed potatoes in the buffet line. No Thanks! If you go to the nearby hospitals to these hotels and ask about the frequency of visitors, you would be surprised at the answer. Not only do the hotels not care about food quality and push the limits with expiration dates, but many of your colleagues have poor hygiene. Order an individual meal or bring snacks.

- **Work for your customers, not the company-** although a company pays your salary, the offices give you sales. The company, on most occasions, are looking out for their best interest. You have to filter what they put out and decide whether it's the best fit for your offices. Many times I tell the office to turn down the companies requests, and advise them on how to best play the situation to their advantage. It ends up working out for all parties. The customer is happy, they take care of me with sales, and the company makes their money. Winner, winner, chicken dinner! Most Pharma companies push too hard, too often. I just regulate that to create a suitable balance for my offices.

- **Never vote Democrat, but never trust Republican-** if you like your job as a pharmaceutical sales representative, that is. If you enjoy the financial perks, free time, and amazing benefits, then do not vote Democrat. The Democratic Party has demonized the pharmaceutical industry as greedy, uncaring, and excessive. I despise politicians. They make any industry their target as long as they are not benefiting from their money. In fact, drug companies give away ALOT, much more than other industries. The fact is that the government wants more of the pharmaceutical proceeds. This is why we operate under a microscope with all of the regulations and compliance in our industry. They love catching us doing something that they consider wrong, like buying a doctor dinner.

Dinner is innocent, but the. Politicians say we are buying prescriptions. But it's ok for a lobbyist to grease their palms for a political favor. Which is really wrong? The Democratic healthcare ideals are based on a generic drug driven system. This would work for a while, but no company is going to do research and development of drugs for free. It takes money to develop and market drugs. I enjoy my job and don't want this industry to go away. If you feel the same, don't vote Democrat.

- **The 3 year rule-** most companies will do everything they can to keep you at the company during the first three years. (sales contests, trips, big bonuses, raises, etc.) However, the next three years they do everything they can to discourage and get rid of you. Notice the contest and bonus potential start to dwindle away. More micro managing, reports, and useless activities. That's your sign to start circulating your resume again. Remember, there is no loyalty among the companies, but among your trust group. Keep them close and always network for the next gig. The large companies will lay you off in a hot minute, even at the holidays. Treasure who gets your loyalty. They have no shame in their game.
- **Pharmaceutical recruiters are like bad realtors**. They don't care about a good fit for you, but rather closing you in a job so they get commission. Many times they won't reveal the number of candidates being considered for a position to you. They string the carrot along in front of you so that in

the event that their top candidate falls through, they have a back up. This is very selfish and inconsiderate to the candidates, but it happens everyday. Never put all of your hope on one position, as you may be interview meat and not be aware. As detailed in my last book, interview meat is the person that gets a courtesy interview without a prayer of closing on the position. Companies need these so that they can reach their HR requirements for number of applicants and diversity. Know how to read it, because it can save you a lot of time and money. Because YOUR time IS money.

- **Exit a company through HR.** When you leave a company, BE SURE that you have reviewed your exit strategy. Use HR to exit and refuse to speak with the manager, unless that person is a friend. Otherwise, they will give you the fast out and jip your proceeds. Hold the company's equipment hostage, subtly, until you receive all of your final payouts. This is especially true at a big Pharma company. They hope you get hit by a bus so they don't have to pay you.
- **The 50% rule.** When interviewing everybody is smiles and golden paths. The hiring manager will say that the territory is capable of producing 60k per year in bonus. So you cut the amount in half, then half again for taxes and that's a more realistic bring home amount. Most managers hyper inflate the bonus to entice reps to come on board. So your 60k is actually 15k in your pants.

- **Avoid romantic encounters within the company.**   Many people attempt to date or hook up within the company, it's always a bad idea. I walked down a scenic path at a beautiful resort in Miami with my boss and a fellow rep to have a private discussion.. Upon reaching the end of the path, we noticed the CEO with one of the obviously beautiful female reps having a discussion, and it wasn't about stock options. We quickly did an about face and walked back to the reception party. My boss said, " that's the things you see that can end your career." We agreed. You may think people don't know or see, but they do. Others have tried to date while working together and special treatment comes up. It's not worth it. Go to another company, then get together. Out of sight, out of mind.
- **Keep your circle small.** Keep the inner circle small. The larger it gets, the greater your risk of sharing information with people that you may not have totally trusted, then the vault is broken. It never fails, that one questionable person will share with someone that nobody trusts, because their personalities had a commonality and they wanted a to make a new friend. You have to know people's motives to consider them in your network. Also from my last book,,see **the five minute rule.** Most people will show you what you need to see in them with a five minute conversation.

- **Never stay on conference calls after they end-** many times a manager may say, " hey John, can you remain on the line after the call ends." Don't do it! These calls are recorded. Tell them you have to go to the restroom and call them back off the conference line.
- **Play the game-** Don't waste time complaining about processes or quotas. This only makes you at troublemaker and eventually a target. Lay low give them what they ask. If they want 6 calls per day and 4 is realistic, make it happen!
- **The loudest person in the room is the weakest-** 15 years of meetings, with 5 different companies, validates that the loudest person at the meetings, is definitely the weakest. Usually it's someone who has self esteem issues that over compensates, or they are trying to be noticed for ladder climbing purposes. Either way, steer clear, no good will come out of it.

Dr. D

Dr. D was a unique Doctor. He ran a family practice doctors office out of an old run down police station. This guy was also a hoarder. There were rooms in this building that had piles of pharmaceutical stuff, such as pens, clocks, staplers, etc. The rumor has it that this guys wife would take these pharmaceutical give aways and sell them on EBAY. Wow! What a great idea, since Viagra pens would sell for 5-10 each! High school kids thought they were cool, so there was a great demand for the good Pharma giveaways. This guy, if he liked you would put you on the map with his prescribing habits. He happened to like me, but his office was disgusting, especially the kitchen. I brought lunch to him a couple of times a month, and without fail, I would see roaches or water bugs in the kitchen. I never ate in that office. It wasn't fit to be declared sanitary enough to draw blood, get a shot, or eat a meal. This guy is the reason is use sanitizer in excess during that time. I would have bathed in it after leaving his office at times.

Once the doctor, who was excessively overweight, smoked, and ate whatever, had to be out for a surgery. He said he would be out for a couple of weeks. I stopped by to leave some forms they requested, and to my surprise, Dr. D was seeing patients, with an IV in his arm. I said " what the hell are you doing back?" He said "I have to pay my ex-wife some extra money, so back to work." He was wearing sweat pants and flip flops and had an IV drip with Hydrocodone in his arm, while seeing patients. The lobby was full. Those people had to be in shock. I was in shock that he had a medical practice. He steps out to take a break and talk with me and my boss. A cigarette lights, then he heads back into the office. My boss is from a wealthy family. When he said Doctor, I bet he thought of the country club or a prestigious practice. He said to me after we returned to the car, " you have just topped the list for the weirdest call I've ever been on with a rep." We both laughed and agreed that Dr. D would never be forgotten by us. I guess that I should have used him as a best practice to share with the sales force.

Dr. D was always asking about one doctor in town, Dr. W. Dr. W owned a piece of land and was approached by a large retail chain to purchase the land, cha-ching!! He was also part owner in a couple of successful restaurants in town. Dr. W was also very well thought of in the medical community. Dr. D went to medical school with Dr. W and was very jealous of him. As a joke, the reps that would visit Dr. D would mention that Dr. W was using a lot of our drug and watch Dr. D fume with jealousy. He once said to me at a lunch, " you know, Dr. W could step in shit, scrape it off hiss joe and it would be gold!" I guess that about sums it up!

Dr. K

Foreign doctors are often very nice to call on. Learning about their story and culture intrigues me. I called on the most unique guy from Lebanon. He is the definition of ADHD. If you can keep his attention for more than 5 minutes, that's an accomplishment! He would allow reps to bring breakfast or lunch, but keeping him in room and not getting distracted was a challenge. I once went to see him and he was scratching his leg and pulling at his pants excessively. I asked him what was wrong. He said "I don't think my dryer is working at home. I dried these pants , but they didn't get dry. " I told him I would take a look at it. We drove over to his house to look at the dryer. I asked him when he changed the filter last. He said, " what filter?" When I opened the lint filter there was enough lint to clothe a small sheep. I told him he should check it every load that it can cause a fire. He shook my hand and told me that I was a great friend. I laughed to myself.

On another occasion I went in to visit Dr. K with information on a new drug. As I sat in his office and detailed him on the drug, he walked into his personal bathroom and began to pee with the door open. In shock, I stopped talking. He said, " no, no, keeping talking." I guess he felt comfortable around me. This ended up happening on more than one occasion. He was so nice and thankful for each visit that I couldn't bring myself to say anything.

Dr. K's staff of 4 people may have a GED, if you combine all of there education. They have the manners of a cornfield worker. My nurse called them about additional information that was needed to get a patient approved. They were so resistant to work, they argued with him about what needed to be completed and the put him on speaker phone and mocked him. Very professional!! This same group ordered lunch for the office on the day that my nurse sponsored a lunch. My nurse ask me to meet him there and I agreed. We both drove about 3 hours each to get to the lunch. The nurse went to the restaurant and picked up the order. There must have been 12 bags of food for 5 people. I said , " what the hell did they order?" My nurse replied that he had no idea. It turns out the office ordered enough food for each of them to have lunch and dinner, which was not the deal. As I walked into the lunch I noticed Dr. K driving away in his truck. I didn't think much of it. Many times people run errands during lunch, but manage to pay the sponsor of the lunch a visit. The nurse and I waited in the lunch room for about 20 minutes. All of the sudden the receptionist came in and informed us that Dr. K was gone for the day. We asked he realized that he had a lunch.

The said, " yes, but he isn't coming back." At the same time is was thinking, " neither are we". This was so rude and a colossal waste of a day. I don't typically work Friday, but this was a great opportunity that turned out to be a flop for me and the nurse. The office should be fat, lazy and happy, as they got 2 free meals out of the deal. I decided that Dr. K's office needed an education and a course in etiquette, so I dropped them from my call list.

It's all about the pay

Pharmaceutical Sales is a great career to pursue, but have another hobby or job to occupy your time. The money is great for the actual hours that people put into the job. There is no immediate gratification of a sale in this job. Your sale today will end up on a report in a couple of months, which is easily forgotten by then. The word sales means that you sold the doctor on your drug. It's more like advisor. As the doctor has many drugs to understand, we as reps usually have 1-3. I flip houses on the side with my wife. My 2-4 hour a day pharmaceutical job finances my house flipping business. These 2 opportunities complement each other from a scheduling standpoint and both are lucrative. My immediate gratification comes from turning a zero house into a hero. The gratification from pharmaceutical sales to me comes from winning. Winning a job over other candidates or winning an award. By the way, being in this business makes me a professional interviewer. I never stop interviewing to keep all of my options open. The record holder for interviews goes to RT. When he officially stops interviewing, I may have a chance at his record. I know a rep that is a fireman on the side, a guy that owns a gym, and someone that has a catering business. Why waste your free time? As there is so much if it in this business. Some reps get so caught up in the numbers and reports that they have no control over. These people only have the pharmaceutical job. Let's face the facts! You have no proof or control over what these companies choose to pay you in bonus. Find something else to do to generate a profit for your family. Regardless of what you are paid in bonus, it is just that, BONUS. We are highly overpaid for what we do, so you will hear no complaints from me. This business is a cash cow for the reps and the companies. Everybody makes a lot of money in the big scheme. I'm in it to win it and make my piece of the pie.

I dedicate this book to my friends and mentors in this business, RT and JH. You guys have taught me a lot about the business. Thanks!

www.ingramcontent.com/pod-product-compliance
Lightning Source LLC
Chambersburg PA
CBHW041750040426

42446CB00001B/3